PR

NO MORE DRAMA — HOW TO MAKE PEACE WITH YOUR DEFIANT KID

BY LISA CAVALLARO

"Over the past 20 years we've learned that *where* our children learn matters to their health, so we've raised our expectations for the classrooms we design and build for them, filling them with daylight, better acoustics, and cleaner, fresher air. Lisa's book is about how, we need to also change the expectations of ourselves as parents, if we want our children to be healthier emotionally. *No More Drama* is her gift to the rest of us who want to help our kids — and ourselves — get and stay on track."

RICK FEDRIZZI
CEO, U.S. Green Building Council

"This book is amazing! It's the real deal for transforming parent-child relationships. I can already feel the relief readers will experience by tuning into Lisa's wisdom and humor on such a challenging subject. Thank you for giving the world this much-needed guide, from someone who's been in the trenches, on how to enjoy parenthood again! If you have kids, do them and yourself a huge favor and read this book!"

JEANNETTE MAW
Good Vibe Coach

"In *No More Drama*, Lisa captures the essence of how to become a happy, effective and healthy parent. Her perspective and exercises teach a person how to create the conditions for joy and wellness in life — as well as in parenting. She entertains and educates in an easy to read and understand dialog with great exercises and achievable objectives. It's a "must read" for all parents — especially those with teenagers!"

MARYANN ROEFARO
Author of *Building the Team from the Inside-Out*

"If overcoming defiance is a journey, this book is the roadmap. Lisa Cavallaro provides real-life parenting strategies to shift yourself out of neutral and confidently into drive. Destination — *No More Drama*!"

ALLISON ZALES
Behavioral Specialist, Choose Change

"As a mom parenting two teenagers who are "out of the box," *No More Drama* is an inspiring story and an effective resource of how to get the joy back in parenting! This is an amazing book that can help any family who is struggling."

SUSAN HYATT
Author and Master Certified Life Coach

NO MORE DRAMA

HOW TO MAKE PEACE WITH YOUR DEFIANT KID

BY LISA CAVALLARO

Cover Design: John Matthews

Interior Design: Heidi Miller

Editing: Kate Makled & Grace Kerina

Author's photo courtesy of Lisa Barcza, Captured Moments Photography

TABLE OF CONTENTS

Even though the future seems far away,
it is actually beginning right now.

MATTIE STEPANEK

INTRODUCTION

"I know you're not working as a therapist any more," my good friend Maria, a social worker, called to say. "But these families really need a *parent coach* — and I think you're perfect!"

"Are you kidding?" I said to Maria. "I have absolutely no idea what a parent coach is, and I highly doubt I'm right for a job I don't even understand."

In my mind, I hadn't come close to mastering this parenting thing, and I didn't know if I would *ever* get there. I mean, don't I have to be an expert parent with my own kids before I can help *someone else* with her parenting issues?

Well — that depends on what you mean by "expert."

In 2006, to me, "expert" meant all kinds of official designations plus degrees and special powers. In my mind, this "parent coach" Maria envisioned was a woman in high heels working from her fancy office, splitting her time between writing parenting textbooks, answering calls from *New York Times* reporters looking for parenting tips, writing a monthly column for *Parent* magazine, and, in her spare time, imparting her wisdom in one-to-one sessions with struggling parents like me.

Okay, as it turns out Maria was a little ahead of me. She recognized that throughout my daughter's pre-teen and teenage years, I was reluctantly, but steadfastly, earning my stripes in the field of parent coaching. Maria knew that some experts' workloads might resemble that of the woman I conjured up. But the expert she sought, the one who could truly help the families walking into her office, was more like me after all ... casually dressed, working from home, enjoying life. Maybe that was who I had become, but hadn't even realized it myself. In other words, the "me" Maria could see now was very different from the woman who first started wearing this "mom" hat.

Something in Common?

As if life isn't busy enough when you're trying to raise a family and have a career, when one of your children becomes defiant, the entire family is affected.

Defiance lived in our home for several years. I have no idea the exact date it moved in, but it's safe to say it took up residence until I made a few changes. Ultimately, *Defiance* figured out its services were no longer needed and gradually departed. Trust me, it was a long journey — one I now help people nip in the bud.

You know, that daughter I mentioned — the one who helped me earn my stripes? She's actually our middle child. One thing I know for sure is that she's the one who made friends with *Defiance* and brought it into our home. It started early — like when Marisa started experimenting with her independence during toddlerhood. People would say what a beautiful smart little girl she was... which was true. But what they didn't see were those battles in our home when this beautiful little girl was in my face with her own ideas about *who* runs things in our home and just *how* to run them.

Meet Defiant

Since I'm not a fan of labels in general, I use the term *defiant* as an adjective — to describe behavior. My daughter was no different from other defiant kids, rebelling against rules and authority, preferring to make her own decisions regarding what to do and how to do it.

In my experience, kids who use defiant behavior like to:

Give "no!" responses

Deliberately annoy

Defy rules

Stomp their feet

Cross their arms

Roll their eyes

Do things that go against authority or directions

This Has Got to Improve

Back then, I would look at this beautiful little child with her captivating blue eyes and I would wonder:

> *Why does she act this way?*
>
> *Why does she push back on everything I do?*
>
> *Will she ever outgrow this behavior?*
>
> *What will I do if her behavior gets worse?*
>
> *Is it even possible for her behavior to get worse?*

These weren't my only worries. They were just the ones I would obsess about *every single day*. And the responses I had at the time were far from encouraging. I was puzzled. I loved this child but I could not understand her — and it wasn't due to my lack of effort.

By a few years later, and after the addition of our third child, my limit had long been exceeded. I was done worrying about the embarrassment of it, and finally marched myself to a therapist. But I didn't get the quick relief I was looking for. So after a few months of therapy, I enrolled myself in Syracuse University's Marriage & Family Therapy program, thinking that a master's degree would help me solve my daughter's problem.

While there may have been a few improvements during my three years of study and practice, my daughter's behavior still wasn't progressing the way I'd hoped.

What's Wrong with This Picture?

It was baffling to me that in earning my graduate degree I had consumed so much information about families, systems, and behavior, yet my own child's behavior was still so far out of line.

I was in my mid forties when I did what I thought was the noble thing to do and left a successful business career to stay home and care for our three kids. Only now that my kids were 17, 14 and 8, I had a master's degree (which had not come easily), and I was *still* feeling like I was not cut out for this "mom" thing. I left a well-paying career for a non-paying one that proved to be more than I could handle — to the point that I would find myself vacillating between verbally or physically lashing out at my child and cursing inward at myself.

Other aspects of my life felt a lot more manageable. Most people who knew me probably wouldn't have guessed I was having those struggles. On the outside, I did my best to present an "I've got it all together" image. But the truth was that I was feeling frazzled and out of control on the inside. This "mom" thing was putting me over the edge in a big way.

"Who am I?" I'd ask myself.

It seemed I'd lost my identity, in addition to the paycheck and the professional challenges I once had and enjoyed. The way I looked at it, I'd given up the rewards of my career for the struggles of parenthood — and regret was setting in.

I'd tell myself that I should have known better. My brother and I weren't the easiest kids to parent and who was I to think that my parents could have two of their four kids push them over the edge, and then all three of mine would be angels?

"Who am I?" That's the question I beat myself up with at the time. But, seriously, who I am is just a normal parent. I was a normal parent struggling and searching for something that would help me help my child. I may have acted like a crazy woman at times, but the craziness was more an expression of my frustration than my overall state of mind.

Sound Familiar?

Maybe you're a little — or a lot — like me when it comes to parenting. I'm guessing you didn't pick this book up for entertainment purposes (although some of my embarrassing parenting stories will definitely make you laugh). If you've read this far into the introduction, then you're probably looking for something. You're probably hoping to find what I was searching for a few years ago — any glimmer of hope. (If that's the case, then you might want to check out the video on my website that will give you that glimmer right now. You can find it at www.lisacavallaro.com)

The good news is that not only did I find that glimmer — I found hope on steroids! What began as an experiment (only because nothing else was working) proved to be the spark I needed to move toward resolving bigger things.

It may seem like your child is more challenge per pound than you'd hoped for — but that's about to change.

Making Your Move

Combinations of medication for children and parents are definitely available. If your intuition is saying this is the right solution for you and your child, then you should probably put this book down and research ADD, ADHD, or anti-anxiety medications. You will find a plethora of medications to choose from.

On the other hand, your gut may be telling you that even though you're not quite sure where it will lead you, simply stepping into this journey is what feels best right now. If this is the case, then stay with me and keep reading, because in this book I'll guide you along the one path that my gut encouraged me to take, and that finally gave me the relief I needed. It gave my daughter room to grow, too.

To give you a heads up, I'll tell about only a fraction of the parenting struggles I faced (embarrassing as they were), then I'll move on to the three simple steps I used that helped me break my cycle of parenting frustration. This process is far from what I thought the answer would be, and it's probably not even close to what you're expecting either.

To get yourself prepared:

> *Rather than* defiant, *what words would you like to use when describing your child?*

What behaviors would you like to notice coming from him or her?

What conversations would you enjoy having with your child?

If you're anything like I was when my daughter Marisa was younger, then you may be struggling to imagine anything different for this particular child of yours. And that's one reason why it's a great idea to start imagining it now. Even if it feels like you're pretending, imagine it anyway. Trust me, if change was possible for my child, then it's possible for yours.

Ready?

Let's do this.

*If everything was perfect, you would
never learn and you would never grow.*

BEYONCÉ KNOWLES

MY STORY

Our son Nick was born four days before our fourth wedding anniversary, and six weeks before our 29th birthdays (yes, my husband Mark and I were born on the same day).

Aside from the fact that we knew absolutely nothing about taking care of kids, let alone raising them, all went really well. We were fortunate to have the tremendous support of our families: both sets of parents and, particularly, my sister Roseanne.

Roseanne, who was just nineteen years old when Nick was born, actually liked kids as she was growing up. This alone was something I could never relate to. But Roseanne was the go-to babysitter in our neighborhood. We still joke about how she was the preferred sitter for a family of three boys and twin girls, all less than five years of age! But my sister thrives amidst the activity of young kids, so much so that she pursued her first college degree in early childhood education. She was a natural.

As for me, I grew up with a football in one hand and a basketball in the other. Our two brothers were closer to my age, so I would spend my days competing against them in one sport or another.

Plans Change

Mark and I originally planned to not have kids. He was always driven and career-focused. I had a comfortable management position at the local power company. We'd been together since our junior year of high school and assumed we would get married, work in our chosen fields, take vacations as often as possible, retire at 62, and then travel more throughout retirement.

But after seeing the fun our niece and nephew brought to their parents' and grandparents' lives (and to us!), I was able to convince Mark that he too could be celebrated on Father's Day if we had our own kid. The rest is history!

So there we were with this beautiful baby boy. Roseanne offered to stay at our house when we brought Nick home. How well I remember the day (seven days after we brought Nick home) when she said she was running to the store. There was no denying the fright on my face as I begged her to stay.

Remember — I really knew *nothing* about taking care of kids. There was one time, before Nick was born, when I changed my niece's diaper. Later, my mother removed the diaper and figured out that I'd put my grandfather's diaper on her. Hey, it was in the closet and that's where the baby diapers were, too. Chalk this up as a learning experience!

And, of course, there were many more learning experiences, like the time I made a doctor's appointment for

Nick because he was having seizures every time I changed his diaper. Mom rushed right over and discovered that the baby wipes I was cleaning him with were lying right next to an outside wall in the house, and they were freezing cold to his little bottom. Poor little guy wasn't having seizures at all — the cold was taking his breath away!

In spite of our inexperience, together Mark and I learned to take great care of our son. As any new parent would agree, it was a huge adjustment just having such a demanding little person in our home. Not that he demanded any more than any other baby, but for two people who were accustomed to caring only for themselves, it took some getting used to.

No doubt about it, Nick made us happy. We enjoyed having our little man around to play with. The kid was always smiling. Give him a ball and he was happy. The more we played, the happier he was. And the happier I was, too. I told Mark I wanted another one.

They're Siblings, Not Clones

Two years and eight months after Nick was born, we were blessed with another beautiful and healthy baby. We named her Marisa — "Mar" from Mark plus "isa" from Lisa. I still remember the high I felt the afternoon after delivering her. We had our son, and now a daughter. We were a family. She was a healthy nine pounds, with daddy's blue eyes and beautiful skin. She was perfect!

This time, when we brought our new baby home from the hospital, I was a pro. Although she was a girl, the basics of caring for her were the same as with Nick. I felt confident — or so I thought!

Going from zero to one kid — even for rookies — was significantly easier than going from one to two. When the adults outnumbered the kid, it was much easier for the two of us to juggle and figure things out. But once Marisa came along, it was more like, "You grab that one and I'll take this one." Overall, it worked. Nick adored his little sister and was quite proud of her.

Marisa was queen in her brother's eyes. He could entertain her for what seemed like a very long time. Let's face it, when you've got two kids under three and they keep themselves busy for ten minutes it's amazing what a mom can accomplish in those 600 seconds. Nick had a knack for acting goofy and getting his baby sister to laugh. It was a sight to see and super helpful to me!

Nick's skill came in handy in later years, too. Our family expanded once more in 1997 with the addition of our beautiful Dina Rose. We call her our best surprise ever. With Nick and Marisa at the ages of 9 and 6 when she was born, we joke that Dina had four parents. Her older siblings wanted to be as involved as they could — that is, after the initial shock of hearing that a little one was on its way.

To quote Marisa, "Nick, can you believe they're doing this to us?"

So here we were — the couple that once aspired to be life-long DINKs (dual income no kids) — blessed with three kids. Dina was the lucky one who got the experienced mother, since by the time she was born I had a much better idea of what I was doing.

To clarify: I had a much better idea of what I was doing when it came to meeting the primary needs of infants and toddlers. In other words, I had the basics of feeding, changing, bathing and schedules completely under control.

But little person *behavior* was a whole different animal!

Only Her Hairdresser Knows for Sure

I recall sitting in the hair salon many times, telling my hairdresser one defiant Marisa story after another — in my attempts to convince her just how difficult this kid was. And every time she'd tell me, "Lisa, don't kill her spirit. She's feisty and that's going to come in handy when she's a teenager and dating." I knew Gina was right. I could see where Marisa's feistiness could be a real asset to her. I just didn't want her using it on *me* anymore!

Then, one day, my charming, dimple-faced, blue-eyed beauty gave my hairdresser her own taste of attitude. Recovering from minor surgery had kept Gina out of work for a few months, so one of her co-workers had cut our hair a few times. Marisa wasn't much for sitting still, so cutting her hair was always a project. The young girl filling in for

Gina was very sweet. She'd just let Marisa squirm and made her cuts between movements. Honestly, I have no idea how she did it.

When Gina returned to work, Marisa was in the chair and, as usual, she was squirming away. Like previous times, Gina asked Marisa to sit still. Marisa's predictable response was to increase the squirming, while adding some eye rolling and "I don't think so" faces.

Finally, Gina raised her voice and told Marisa, "Look. If you don't stop moving, I'm not going to cut your hair and you're going to have to find someone else to do it."

Without hesitation, Marisa responded, "Don't worry, Gina. I already have someone in mind."

Gina was totally unprepared for the comment. No doubt, Marisa had loved Gina's co-worker, who'd let her roam about freely in the chair. Given a choice, Marisa would go back to the co-worker in a heartbeat.

Maybe the correct parenting response would have been for me to tell my daughter to apologize for her comment to Gina, but that was not going to happen. I felt vindicated! After listening to all my defiant Marisa stories, Gina now had one of her very own. Hah! Sweet!

There was something validating about having someone else experience the feelings I felt every day. If only someone else experiencing them could have taken my uncomfortable feelings away, but it didn't.

I would begin each morning with a prayer that Marisa would give me a break for just one day — that she'd back her little self off and behave like I needed her to. For just one day, it would have been nice to have her go with the flow, be agreeable, and co-operate with me. But, then again, if that prayer were ever answered for even one day, I would have wondered what was wrong. Because that kid had her own ideas, and they were *never* aligned with mine.

The Breaking Point

It's probably a good thing that I don't remember the details that precipitated this one particular day. I do, however, remember that evening. We had put the kids to bed, and Mark and I were enjoying our glasses of wine. Or shall I say it started out as "enjoying" until I finally started talking openly about the humungous elephant in our home.

It was no news to Mark — or anyone else in the family, for that matter — that Marisa and I were butting heads, big time. It was an all day, every day kind of thing — and it got pretty ugly at times.

Finally, on this night, I admitted out loud to my husband that there were times when I did not like my own daughter. Making this admission was a dual-edged sword for me. As if the discomfort of feeling it were not bad enough, saying it out loud to my daughter's other parent was humiliating. I hated feeling this way and I knew he couldn't even relate to it.

Mark was and still is a terrific dad. He loves his kids and they love him right back. My "struggle years" were also what he calls his "lost years," because he maintained a focus on growing our business (something he did exceptionally well) and was too exhausted for much else.

When it came to parenting, I was the one on the front lines. Mark really didn't see a lot of what was going on and after dealing with business all day long, the last thing he wanted to face was family drama.

But we did agree on one thing that night: Something needed to change. And the next day I called a therapist.

Isn't She Lovely?

I found it puzzling that the first therapist I worked with focused each session on me — my relationships and my ideas — when the problem I was having was with my daughter. Then, more than a year later, when another well-regarded therapist made an unexpected comment, I began to wonder. I met with this woman because I wanted her to fix Marisa's behavior. Yet after telling her all about my child, she said:

"I'm sure your daughter's lovely. I prefer to work with you."

I thought the woman was crazed at first — at least very mistaken. I assured her that my daughter was in fact very lovely to the eye, but her behavior was far from lovely. The woman chuckled but never wavered in her plan.

Although I disagreed with the therapist, I found her knowledge appealing. She seemed to understand kids and had a lot of experience with difficult ones. With a terrific sense of humor, she seemed to have the kind of kid smarts I could benefit from. So even though I disagreed with her strategy, I stuck around — for probably forty sessions over a three-year span.

Parenting and Weight Loss Aren't All That Different

It was 2008 and I was by then a master certified life coach, working with very smart people who wanted to lose weight permanently. After teaching clients some basic principles and then guiding them along as they experimented with their new tools, they realized amazing results.

I still had this problem with my daughter. I had already tried everything — read all the books, gone to therapy, even earned a master's degree in family therapy — and the situation was definitely better, but not better *enough*. Marisa's behavior was still an issue in our home and I wanted it to be different.

Finally, one day, it hit me.

I started thinking of the techniques I used with clients and wondered: What would happen if I used the same techniques with my parenting dilemma?

Don't Believe Everything You Think

Not surprisingly, people trying to lose weight can be especially hard on themselves. They think their ability to lose weight depends on things like:

The genes they inherited

Their ability to lose weight in the past

Finding the right diet

Something I would often repeat to them was: "Don't believe everything you think."

It was easy for me to see that if they believed their genes made a difference ... and they believed their past prevented them from losing weight now ... and they believed that they needed to find the right diet ... then their success with permanent weight loss was doomed.

So long as my clients believed they needed to control something they didn't have control over — like genes, the past, and the right diet — then they wouldn't be successful.

Okay, so how could I apply this to parenting my daughter?

What did I currently believe that might be preventing my success? Actually, I believed a lot of things about Marisa. I believed she was stubborn, bossy, and demanding and my list could go on. It wasn't a pretty list, and all I could see was my frustration.

It took some time, but when it hit, it hit me big! "Wait a minute, Lisa! What would you tell your client if *she* was complaining about her stubborn, bossy, and demanding child?"

Hmmm ... Right! I did not like this!

The therapists were right.

This whole parenting issue was really about me.

It was not Marisa's fault.

Let Me Rephrase That

I must have been feeling the same initial shock that a lot of my clients felt. I finally realized that waiting for someone or something else to change was a big waste of my time. It also fried my insides and made me obsessive.

All along, I'd been searching for something or someone that could control my kid, when all I really had control over — and was *ever* going to have control over — was myself.

Coming to grips with this fact was not something that took place overnight. It took me time and continuous effort. Let's face it — this fact was in my face for a long time. Both therapists knew it. My husband knew it. My hairdresser knew it. And I knew this kind of stuff when it came to my clients. But it took a while for me to see it in the mirror.

I finally realized that I was holding on to two beliefs that turned into my greatest roadblocks to having peace, or at least a less defiant kid:

1. I need Marisa to behave.

2. I need Marisa to respect me.

Those beliefs always sounded so reasonable. Kids are supposed to behave and they're supposed to respect us. I believed that ... but the fact was that mine did not behave and she did not respect me. Believing I needed those two things, that I didn't have or control, was not working for me.

As a firm believer in an ideal that includes obedient and respectful kids, I struggled with the idea of changing my beliefs. And I finally did. As painful as they were at first, I adopted two new beliefs:

1. I need to behave.

2. I need to respect myself.

Taking the focus off my kids and putting it on myself was about as easy as making a braid out of my daughters' hair (I stink at braids). So let's just say that when it comes to both, I'm *still* a work in progress! Attempting to control my own behavior and learn some self-respect was a full-time job for a girl (me!) not used to this sort of thing.

My impression of parenting was much like what's now known in the business world as *micromanaging*. I thought it was my responsibility to get my kids to do things — the *right things*. What the heck is the *right thing* anyway? Is it always the same?

Looking back now, I can laugh at myself. But, at the time, I wanted to cry. It felt like a lot of pressure. I was constantly trying to figure out a strategy for getting my kids to act respectfully, eat the right foods, hang with the right people, attend the right parties, say the right things, score high grades, play certain sports, blah, blah, blah. I thought that was a reflection of who I was as a parent, and I so desperately wanted to do it *right*.

I know I'm not alone here. Maybe this stuff makes you uncomfortable, too. It's as if there's this package of goods that we innocently buy into — a package that tells us our kids require lots of direction and if we parents don't give it to them, then they're doomed for lives of failure. Or maybe your beliefs are a little different, but they still include a very clear picture of what *success* looks like when raising a family.

Don't get me wrong — I'm a big believer in achieving, making healthy choices, hanging with awesome people, and having a plan. I just no longer believe that there's only one way to get these things, or, further, that my kids need to believe in the *same* things I do in order to create and enjoy happy, healthy, and successful lives. In fact, raising them to develop and respect an internal compass will save them a lot of pain at some point, too!

It took me years to figure this out. And, God knows, when anyone interfered with my timeline, it only messed things up. I was the kind of kid who accepted advice only if I asked for it, and anything uninvited or unsolicited simply complicated things and added to my frustration. (Perhaps you're thinking that Marisa didn't just get her defiance from the sky and trees — and you're probably right!) ☺

Let me add my heartfelt disclaimer: *I totally recognize and appreciate that the adults in my life who tried to make things easier for me by encouraging certain choices and paths did so because they cared about me and they cared about my future. It feels awesome knowing that they cared so much that it moved them to action.*

I want to help my kids too — which is why I made every effort to control their choices regarding most things. In my mind, I knew what was best for them and I had my ideas on how to help them get those things.

But there was backfiring going on all over the place before I realized it.

Marisa's defiant behavior was less about her character and more a rebellion to my over-parenting. The kid just didn't want so many of my opinions in her face all day long. Could I blame her? Well, obviously, I did — for a long time! But more control created more backtalk and more defiance.

I couldn't see it then, but it's so very clear today.

My energy in those early parenting days was all about control.

How can I control these kids?

How can I get them to do what I need them to do?

How can I control their friends, their grades, their activities and everything else in their lives?

How can I teach them to control themselves?

Control. Control. Control.

These days, just thinking about it makes me cringe.

Example is leadership.

ALBERT SCHWEITZER

STEP ONE
AIM HIGH

The one and only way to "teach" kids how to lead happy, fulfilling lives is to show them how it's done. We can tell them all we want about the things they "have to" do, but, let's face it, we hated getting all that unsolicited advice from people when we were kids. It never really made sense to me when my father would tell me that whatever I did reflected on him. I mean, I sort of got it... but still I thought I was responsible for my choices, so why would those not-so-brilliant ones make *him* look bad?

The truth is that our kids' choices make us look bad only if we allow it. Once we come to the conclusion that our kids need to experiment with life (the same way that we did) in order to fully experience who they are, then those very choices suddenly become all about them ... and zippo about us!

When it comes to directions, what kids need to hear from us is very different from what we might think. They don't need to be told what to do, how to do it, where to do it, who to do it with, or when to do it.

All they need is our vote of confidence that we believe they will figure it out!

If this doesn't make sense to you, then let's go back a few years...

Can you recall a time in your childhood when you did something, or wanted to do something, but an authority figure (parent, teacher, grandparent, trusted adult) didn't approve? What happened?

It's probably a safe bet to say that you were feeling neither supported nor free to make your own choices. Maybe you even felt some shame in there. And you most definitely sensed their lack of faith in you and your abilities.

What else? Did it feel controlling — like people didn't think you had what it took to succeed? Did it seem like they thought you needed them to make your decisions for you? Or even that they simply wanted to exercise their will over yours?

Maybe these well-meaning folks thought you needed their help, or maybe they were just trying to protect you. Either way, did it feel good?

Of course it didn't feel good. It never feels good when we sense disapproval coming from anyone — let alone the very people whose approval we crave most.

Our kids want our approval just like we wanted the approval of the trusted adults in our lives. Sure, there are times when giving that approval seems extra challenging — but that's what it is — a challenge. It's not impossible.

Approval doesn't have to come in the form of agreement. Even when we can't agree with what they've done or are considering doing, we can at least contribute something to the conversation that lets them know that we believe in *them*!

When you really think about this, it opens the door to all kinds of possibilities for conversations with our kids.

Simply conveying our faith in kids eliminates the need for what I consider to be...

The Top Ten Parent Moves That Backfire with Kids:

1. Saying, "I wouldn't have done it that way."

2. Asking, "What were you thinking?"

3. Commenting, "You should have asked me first."

4. Saying, "I told you so."

5. Declaring, "You deserved it."

6. Head-shaking.

7. Finger-pointing.

8. Rule-making.

9. Punishing.

10. Saying, "I'm disappointed."

Maybe you're looking at this list and noticing that even as an adult, you don't like it when someone — anyone —

does these things to you? Yes, exactly! That's my point. No one likes these things being done to them, and kids are no different.

But, for some reason, we continue to believe that kids *need* these things, and we parents are the ones who *need* to give it to them. We should probably think again!

If the items on this list made us want to rebel when we were kids, then let's reconsider using them with our own kids.

The fact is that babies come into this world as innocent little humans with clean slates. Then we adults take it upon ourselves to confuse their basic need for food, clothing, and shelter with their non-need for imparting our worldly wisdom. The truth is that they don't need the latter — because they are perfectly capable of figuring things out for themselves.

So the reason we let our kids know that we have faith in them is because it helps them. They came into this life wanting to live it, and when someone as important to them as a parent continually lets them know that they have all they need to succeed, then they feel inspired. Doing this lets the child know you're not expecting perfection. More importantly, it lets them know that you love them even when they're not perfect. When a parent does this for a child, it's like giving the child carte blanche to live life — complete with mistakes — knowing full well that no matter what, the support of the most important adults in their lives will always be there.

This is huge for kids!

But there's another reason why having faith in our kids' abilities to make their own choices and lead their own lives is extremely important — and this reason is what the rest of this book is dedicated to enabling.

Most folks are as happy as they make up their minds to be.

ABRAHAM LINCOLN

Begin with Your Happiness in Mind

When I first began coach training, one of my mentors, Brooke Castillo, told me that the greatest gift I could give to anyone was my own happiness. I liked the sound of her statement — a lot — but I never really acted on the words until much later. And parenting is one of the best subjects to apply this thinking toward.

My happiness is a great gift to my kids, because when I take responsibility for creating my own happiness, I take that responsibility off the shoulders of my kids. I don't need my kids to do certain things, or do things a certain way, in order for me to be happy — because I am already happy. It's also a gift to my kids because they see me modeling what "happy" looks like, so it gives them an idea of how to do their own version of "happy."

So if this is beginning to seem a little weird to you at this point, then you're right where I was when I first thought about this. Please hang in there and keep reading. I promise it will make more sense later!

This book began with a glimpse into my struggles as a parent and it progressed on to why kids really don't need what we, as adults, have been trying to jam down their throats. Now we're getting into the good stuff! We're moving away from parent "problems" and into parent solutions.

In my first weeks of grad school, one of my professors told me I was going to make an amazing solution-focused therapist and at that point, I wasn't totally sure what she meant. But now, as a coach, I get it.

I got totally distracted doing therapy on the problems in clients' lives. Focusing on pain in people's lives only seemed to cause more pain for them. But there's something about working with solutions that really jazzes me. It just makes sense to think about, focus on, and imagine solutions — even if the only reason to do it is because it feels *way better*!

The key to helping our kids move out of their challenging behavior patterns is to add some excitement to the mix. If we keep looking for problems with our kids, we'll find them for sure. But that's not what we want. What we want is to see all the good that's inside them and around them — and in order to *see* it, we have to *look* for it!

How do you look for goodness in your child?

For me, finding the goodness in my daughter started with getting happier in my own life. As I focused on getting happier, my perspective of her seemed to change. For one thing, I spent more time thinking about things that made me happy, and less time on things about her that bothered me.

It was almost as if I didn't have time to think about what she was doing... and I don't mean that in a neglectful way. I cared about her and what she was doing and I was still very present in her life, but I didn't dwell on her actions. Big difference!

It's funny what ended up happening.

If you're familiar with Dr. Wayne Dyer, then you've probably heard him say that when you change the way you look at things, the things you look at change. Let me tell you, he is not kidding!

Not that I used his words as my motto or anything, but I did change how I was looking at Marisa. She. Did. Change. (Or was it my experience of her that changed?)

I was finally beginning to experience her as the delightful teenager she was.

What did I do differently? In a word, I did less.

In my mind, I set higher expectations for Marisa. I didn't expect her to display the little hissy fits that I used to expect daily. Instead, I began to look forward to and appreciate some of the exceptionally entertaining things about this kid. She actually created and ran her own fantasy conglomerate from our home, beginning when she was just eight years old. I didn't appreciate it back then, but I was able to take pleasure in her enthusiasm for business as she grew older. (And as I grew more willing!)

I knew that there were so many positive things about this kid that I hadn't been able to see for a very long time — and I made it my mission to look for them.

Obviously, that young mind of hers was brilliant in how she focused on her pretend businesses. She ran a hotel chain. She was a logistics specialist arranging coast-to-coast freight transportation. She sold food products (like her

Dad). She was a travel agent. And there may have been more. This kid had employees, vendors, phone meetings, and forms — lots of forms!

There were so many forms, and they were hysterical to read. She would modify the forms my husband used in his business and suit them to her businesses. Her teacher once wrote a note to Marisa on her husband's stationery, and Marisa really liked the husband's initials so she used his initials as the name of her conglomerate. She even wrote about EGW Enterprises for one of her college projects. Such an imagination!

At this point, you might be thinking, "Gee, this is the first time in this book that Lisa had anything good to say about her daughter." And you'd be right. So if you're feeling this shift in perspective, can you even imagine how different this shift felt for me?

It was different and amazing at the same time. What's not always clear about *focus* is that we really aren't as great at multi-tasking as we think we are, and that's a really good thing here. Since we really can truly focus on only one thing at a time, in this case the positive aspects of our kids, what we will see is just that — the positive aspects of our kids! We get to see what's good and great and entertaining and funny and brilliant about them. And that may have been a long time coming.

Children are educated by what the grown-up is and not by his talk.

CARL JUNG

Kids Learn from What We Do
They don't give a crap what we tell them.

I was absolutely insane to think I could tell Marisa not to scream at me, when I would also scream at her. Who was I to think I could tell her to "give it up" when I would not let things go? Chronologically, I was the adult. Biologically, I was the parent. Ironically, I was behaving like neither.

When I would tell Marisa to do something, she would consistently not follow my directions. Instead, she would feed whatever emotion I was putting out as I gave her those directions. And my emotions were *rarely* good!

What I was typically putting out was anger, and I could always count on her response to be something that would make me even angrier. She was responding to the conditions I created, which actually meant she was a very sensitive and responsive individual. The conditions simply weren't generating a positive feedback loop yet.

It was as if she had a built-in hypocrite-detector letting her know what an idiot I was to act one way and expect her to act differently. Not that kids aren't capable of finding their way with minimal guidance from us, but if we want them to grow into responsible adults, it makes sense to show them how it's done!

It's not like I did this deliberately — or even consciously. It just came naturally. (Lucky me, right? Why couldn't it be hip-hop dancing or picking winning lottery numbers that comes naturally to me?)

Exercise

1. Is there a particular behavior in your child that angers you most?

2. How do you respond to this behavior when your child does it?

3. What emotion do you think you might be feeling when this happens?

4. Now it's Prep time!

   a. What *better-feeling emotion* would you like to feel the next time your child does this behavior (e.g., compassion, optimism, love, anything that feels better than your answer to #3 above)?

   b. What thought could you *think* that will allow you to feel the better-feeling emotion the next time you're in that moment?

Note: If you've ever tried to change a habit before, then you know how challenging it can be. Just keep in mind that repetition is key. Repetition is how we developed our habits of thought in the first place — and that's how we change them, too. As you continue practicing step 4 above, you are dropping your old thought pattern and the associated feelings you had as a result — and you are creating a habit that includes a better feeling for you. When you feel better, you take good-feeling actions. (Hmmm ... If only I knew this a few years ago!)

Change is the law of life.

And those who look only to the past or present are certain to miss the future.

JOHN F. KENNEDY

Leave the Past Behind
Unless it inspires you!

Any one of us who has had a challenging kid would have no problem finding things to complain about. Whether we, or the kids, were responsible for those things, plenty was done that we wish we could change. The truth is, we probably created the issue right alongside the kid who committed the deeds. But, seriously, why bother thinking about it? In the words of my younger brother after he totaled my first car: "It's done. It's over. Can't change it. Move on."

A client once told me that her son reminded her of her nephew — a beautiful and smart young man — but her son was also uncontrollable. Her nephew was difficult as a child, and in his teenage years chose a life of drugs and crime. My client had a very close relationship with her nephew — as if she was a second mother to him — and each time her nephew got into trouble, the woman felt less effective in her role as an aunt *or* parent. She noticed similarities between her nephew and her own son. They obviously shared some of the same genes. They looked very similar to each other, and some of their talents were even the same.

Even though her son was much younger, each time he acted out, she saw him growing up to have the same life her nephew chose. She was so fearful of this happening that she was especially hard on her son. Each time he did something she disagreed with, her plan was to punish him with twice what she thought he deserved.

Once this client made a conscious decision to see her nephew and her son as two very different people, she could see differences between them. We worked on leaving those past experiences with her nephew behind. Even though she cared deeply for her nephew, she was not his parent, and was certainly not responsible for how he lived his life. She was especially relieved when she came to the realization that her nephew's parents were not at fault either. The nephew, she later understood, made his own decisions that reflected his own course in life. It was no one else's job to change those decisions.

Exercise

1. Is there anyone in your life whom you consciously or sub-consciously compare your child with?

2. How would you feel right now if you saw your child and this other person as two distinctly different people whose choices have absolutely nothing to do with each other?

3. List ten differences that exist between your child and this other person.

Life is really simple, but we insist on making it complicated.

CONFUCIUS

Parenting Should Not Be Difficult
If only I believed that when they were born.

Have you checked out the parenting section in the bookstore lately? There are many shelves and sections of books on the topic. You can find anything you want (and more) on the myriad of different philosophies of parenting. You can learn all about the *shoulds* and *should nots* of how to parent your child.

If you'd rather not read parenting books, you can always use your fingers to find the latest information regarding how to parent your child. I know for a fact that the World Wide Web has a plethora of information available on defiant kids — because I researched the topic plenty during my struggle years and then again as I wrote this book. The only difference between then and now is that even more information is circulating the Internet and even more books have been written.

So, why am I writing one more?

I am not writing this book because I think the bookstore or the Internet needs one more parenting book. I happen to think that if a parent is searching for information on how to better guide or understand their child's behavior, then they certainly have enough information out there to choose from.

The reason I'm writing this book is because I know there are parents like me out there who have read all the books and perused most of the online information — and they're still looking. They want something different — something that *feels* more doable. We know from experience that trying to change and/or help our kids through behavior struggles is exhausting and has gotten us nowhere so far.

The parents this book appeals to are open-minded. If adopting a less-complicated style of parenting means going against the grain of traditional parenting, then it's fine with them.

How do I define "traditional" parenting? Traditional parenting tends to focus directly on those receiving the parenting, namely the children. In my parenting research, I was able to find loads of information on how to understand and control my children's behavior. As interesting and informative as all that information was, it didn't give me what I wanted ... or needed.

Exercise

Regardless of your child's behavior today, think of how you *want* to see your child.

On a piece of paper, list the character traits you *want* to notice in him or her?

What conversations would you *like* to have together?

Which activities would you see him or her taking part in?

What are some of the things you would laugh about together?

I love it when people doubt me.

*It makes me work harder to
prove them wrong.*

DEREK JETER

Limits Are for Speed
They're not for hopes and dreams and abilities.

In 2008, as crazy as the idea was for someone with minimal swimming ability, I signed up for a triathlon. I reasoned that since I had eleven months to learn and practice, then I'd be fine. Of course, I'd heard all the comments about how the swim portion is the most challenging of the race. And how doing the right breathing is tough to learn. And let's not forget the stroke itself: *1-2-3-breathe* was something that required focus, too. And how about the kick? There's a right way, and a wrong way.

Bless those retired people who swam at the pool early each morning. They were my coaches and inspiration, and answered any ridiculous little question I threw their way. They'd been swimming at the community college pool for years, and filled me in on all the math I needed to get some bearings — 18 down-and-backs made a half-mile, which was approximately how long the swim portion of the triathlon was going to be.

About one month into my training, my daughter Dina (who was a casual swimmer and 11 years old at the time) had a day off from school and wanted to come to the pool with me. I'll never forget that day!

We walked up to the shallow end of the pool and Dina asked me, "How many laps to make a half-mile?" As soon as I got the words "18 down-and-backs" out of my mouth, she was in the water heading for the deep end. And the kid did not stop until she had finished her 18 down-and-backs!

As someone very much in the struggle stage of my training, I was amazed! How did she do that? Did she not know how hard that was? After all, I certainly knew how hard it was!

Hah! Look where all that knowledge got me! It was as hard as I expected it to be. Maybe harder.

Dina's instinct to jump right into that challenge was the best thing she could have done for herself. Because if I had gotten hold of her ear, I would have filled it with all the difficulties associated with swimming "that far for so long!" I would have told her how hard it was for me and how slow the normal learning curve is. I would have told her to look out for the guy in the lane next to her, because he often crosses over. I would have told her that it's okay to take breaks (not that it isn't). And I would have introduced her to the lifeguard and told her not to be shy in asking for help. (Not that that's a bad idea either.)

But give that kid credit. She jumped in and she did it — without even realizing what a big deal it was. For her, it was something she wanted to do. She had no reason to believe she wasn't capable of doing it. So she just started ... and succeeded.

Maybe you're thinking right now of a similar situation between you and your child. Isn't it amazing the things they can do when they don't doubt their ability to do it?

When we put our two cents in between our kids and their desires, what happens is that while we may think we're setting them up for success, what we're unintentionally doing is giving them reasons why they should expect difficulty and possibly even failure.

We try to protect our kids from making the same mistakes we make — as if that's even possible.

They actually require far less direction from us than we think. Kids continually amaze me! Just when I think they've done it all, they find a way to accomplish more. And they know it. It feels great to them when they're doing it. They want to do more and it's easier for them to do it when we step aside, express our faith in their ability, and let them figure it out.

Exercise

1. Think of something that challenges you. Maybe it's a physical activity or a sport. Maybe it's a fear of something, like heights or bees or animals.

2. What are you tempted to say to your child about this thing?

3. Now imagine your child having an interest in the thing that challenges you. What can you tell yourself about your child that will help you feel more confident in his or her ability to figure things out?

Kids are smart. Knowledge is power.
Let them figure things out.

Don't turn into that grown-up who
they won't come to.

LAUREN MYRACLE

They Know

And they're more capable than we think.

When our son Nick was 13 years old, he and I were driving alone in the car one afternoon. I thought it was the perfect time to talk to him about one of his friends. This particular character wasn't one of his closest buddies, but they were spending more and more time together and I figured it was my place to "warn" Nick about the dangers of hanging with this kid.

So I basically went into a monologue about the 14-year-old, listing all the things I heard he was doing, which were things that I certainly didn't want my kid doing. I made sure to include the old "guilty by association" lesson, too, just so Nick would realize that hanging with this guy could prove damaging to his own reputation if he kept the friendship going.

But the lesson was all mine when, after listening to my rampage, Nick very calmly said, "I know all this, Mom, and I know what I'm doing." He wasn't disrespectful in his delivery. He was just stating the fact that he was well aware of the situation and that he could handle it.

And in total non-Lisa fashion, I'm not sure why, but I accepted his response.

In his very young, but mature way, Nick was telling me that things didn't have to be so black or so white. There was plenty of gray space associated with this friend of his, and Nick cleverly knew how to navigate that space. I may not have recognized the gray or Nick's ability, but Nick sure did.

There I was, trying to push my anxiety onto my kid and instead of taking on my insanity, Nick eased it.

Sometimes it's hard for us adults to realize that children so young can have so much in the way of smarts. Kids know things innately. We're the ones who think we need to fill their little heads with information. And we think we need to keep repeating the information over and over again until they get it and do what we're telling them.

Only what ends up happening is that kids get annoyed with the repetition and the unsolicited advice and then they begin to rebel against it.

This I know from my own teenage years!

You don't learn to walk by following rules.

You learn by doing, and by falling over.

RICHARD BRANSON

Yesterday's Rules
How do they feel today?

What if you put the rulebooks aside and did what felt right to you?

What if, instead of listening to other people's opinions about what you should do with your child, you trusted yourself enough to do what felt right to you?

What would happen if you cared about one thing and one thing only: how you feel?

What if you didn't make how you feel be about your kids but you made it be about you?

If all this seems too strange and "out there" to even fathom believing, then put yourself in the child's position. What kind of authority do *you* benefit most from?

> *Do you like rules and regulations?*
>
> *Do you like it when bosses or the government dictate what you need to do?*
>
> *In other words, do you like being controlled?*
>
> *Do rules, regulations and consequences bring out the best in you?*

If you're like most people, then you're cringing right now at the thought of someone attempting to pull your strings. And yet, for some reason, we think as parents that it's our job to control the decisions, actions, and experiences of our kids. What makes us think that our kids are so different from us that they would welcome this behavior from adults?

We think this way because most of us have been taught that sharing all we know with our kids is our responsibility as parents, and it's also what loving parents *should* do.

It's really worth your while to take a few minutes to think about the beliefs you hold regarding parenting. The purpose of this exercise is not to identify any right or wrong beliefs (nothing is right or wrong here), but to understand what drives your thoughts and actions behind your parenting decisions. (As an example, I used to believe that good parents sacrificed things they wanted so that they could send their kids to certain schools.) What beliefs influence you most?

Exercise
Things "Good" Parents Do

1. _____

_____

2. _____

_____

3. _____

_____

4. _____

_____

5. _____

_____

6. _____

_____

7. _____

_____

8. _____

_____

9. _____

_____

10. _____

_____

Life is largely a matter of expectation.

HORACE

Expect Good Things
And that is what you will see.

With all the parenting books, experts, and information in circulation, it's easy to think you don't know what to do with your own child. I know, because I've been there. You hear of a new diagnosis (with 3 or 4 catchy-sounding letters) whose main symptoms are *exactly* what you notice in your kid. So you buy the book, read it, tell your partner, your friends, and possibly a therapist about it. You may even get this condition added to your child's school record, so that everyone in school knows that your child displays these symptoms and has "limitations."

If this scenario sounds familiar, please know that I'm not knocking it. I'm quite familiar with it, in fact, because I've lived it. And it didn't help.

For some reason, I felt it was my parental duty to inform teachers who had my son in their classes that his sister was very different. I never had to raise the topic of Marisa's academics because she was always a conscientious and high-achieving student. But I did feel the need to warn them about her behavior. In other words, I set the expectation for her teachers that my daughter would be a problem in class.

As fate would have it, Marisa would present more of a challenge to her teachers — and much of what she would do in the classroom would mirror what she did at home. She would look for (and find) any way to get around the rules, and she would not be shy about questioning certain teachers whenever they came to her with any type of constructive criticism.

Ironically, this makes me think of a similar situation, one I handled very differently.

When Nick was very young, we had his hearing tested and found that he only had 17 percent hearing in one ear. I very intentionally did not share this information with his schools, coaches, or anyone else for that matter — including his grandparents and Nick himself — until I finally mentioned it to family when Nick was in high school.

My thought was that if people knew, they might treat him differently — especially his teachers and coaches, and definitely his well-meaning relatives. I was worried that they might unknowingly encourage him to not use that ear. So I did my best to make it a non-issue. My husband and I knew, and that was that.

Interestingly enough, without receiving any special treatment, Nick has always heard and spoken as well as anyone with 100 percent hearing.

Was it my obligation to give the schools information regarding my son's hearing? Some would argue that it was, but I felt strongly that things would work out best for Nick if this one thing were kept under wraps.

How differently I handled those two situations: Marisa's behavior and Nick's hearing. I intentionally set the school's expectation very differently for each — because I was the one who had very different expectations for these two kids!

Innately, I felt confident that Nick's situation would work out best for him if we did not shine a light on it. Yet, my lack of confidence with Marisa's situation led me in various directions searching for answers.

Confidence — and lack of it — was what made the difference!

Having the confidence to make parenting decisions can make a world of difference for our kids. And for us, too!

I didn't realize it then but I definitely do now. The way I felt about these two situations with my kids felt extremely different to me.

Thinking about and explaining Marisa's behavior was exhausting. I was probably boring the daylights out of my polite listeners, but that didn't stop me. I just kept shining a light on something that I wanted to change, without realizing that all the negative attention I was giving it was actually making the situation worse.

As my two very different experiences demonstrate, expectation is everything! What we expect sets the stage for what we experience and, as I learned, setting a negative expectation is far from helpful!

Thankfully, it's never too late to raise the old expectation bar. Even though you might be thinking that there is no way you can raise your expectations while remaining realistic, let me suggest something that worked for me:

1. First, set expectations for yourself as parent.

2. Then set expectations for your child.

Side note: Both will be easier than you think!

Heads up—These Next Few Pages Are All About *You!*

If someone were to ask you to describe yourself, how would you respond? Would your answer focus more on your career, education, health, partner, and child status? Or would you give them a description of things that light you up? (Again, there are no rights or wrongs — just good-to-know info!)

My experience, both with asking and answering this question, is that most (if not *all*) of us tend to define ourselves by the things we do and the roles we play. We're so busy in our lives that we rarely take the time to even find out who we are at our deepest inner cores. In fact, even pondering the notion that I even had an inner core seemed foreign to me at first.

But I do have one — and you do, too. You're more than just a parent or a partner or an employee or a business owner. Even if you cannot describe what else you are, know that whatever it is, you are constantly evolving. Life in and of itself is about growth and we're all here to grow.

We're not here to be perfect or change the world. We're here to grow.

This may be another one of those statements that make you go "Hmmmm ... I'm not sure about that?"

But think about it for a few seconds and notice how it feels. When you think that you don't have to be a perfect person (or a perfect parent), and you don't have to create any great changes in the world, do you feel any sense of relief?

If it does feel like less of a load on your shoulders, then it *is* true for you. That's what using your intuition is all about — trusting your own gut reactions to let you know what's right for *you*.

You can't get your gut reactions out of a book, and you won't find them online either. And other people can't tell you. You can, however, experience them in your body by experimenting with what feels good and what doesn't. Getting in the habit of noticing how you feel about the thoughts you think can — and will — prove priceless in your parenting and in all facets of your life!

Paying attention to your gut reactions can also prove extremely helpful in setting expectations for yourself and for your child. You've probably figured out by now that I'm going to recommend that you make lists of your expectations. I'm also recommending that your lists contain items that feel right to you. Of course, you'll be able to separate what feels right from what doesn't just by how it feels.

So if you want to create an expectation for yourself *and* it feels good, then listing it would be a good idea.

If you want to believe you already know some of the answers you're searching for, but you really don't believe that yet, then don't write it on your list. Play around with the words a bit. Does it feel like relief when you think that you are *capable of* finding your own answers?

This might be a great beginning point. When you think and speak in terms of what you're capable of, it feels good to you *and* it takes your focus off what doesn't feel so good. No matter what your relationship is with what you want (i.e., how close you are to getting what you want), when you think about your capabilities, you're actually getting closer.

When you *think* you're capable and you see yourself as being capable, then you *feel* capable and you *act* in ways that prove you're capable.

Now would be a great time to dismiss any information to the contrary.

The old "I'll believe it when I see it" motto is actually an overused backward representation of what's really going on.

If you don't believe it first, then you'll never be able to see it — even when it's smack in front of your face!

I never thought I was smart enough to do the things I wanted to do. I convinced myself of that because my high school grades averaged in the upper seventies. Forget the fact that I passed every class without opening the books. Forget that my math scores were over 95. Forget the fact that the main reason I didn't study was because my father told me to and I was a hardheaded rebel. I chose to judge my intelligence based on my high school grades.

One problem that went along with my choices about studying in high school was that no matter what I did that might have demonstrated that I was smart, I still considered myself "not smart *enough*." I was stuck on the old proof I'd created, to the point that I could not see that earning a master's degree, magna cum laude, while running a household with three kids and accumulating 500 client-contact hours, was definitive proof that my old belief required updating.

This is one of those points so worth repeating: **If you want something to happen, you have to believe it *can* happen *first*!**

And, just as you're thinking right now, this goes for more than only parenting. When you look at yourself as a person capable of so much more than you previously realized, your mind becomes filled with possibilities. Any troubles you may have been experiencing with your child occupy your mind less than ever before — because thinking in terms of possibility is more exciting.

Again ... you guessed it! When you think less about problems with your child, you have fewer problems to think about.

Getting back to those expectations. I've taken the liberty of suggesting a few expectations to get you started and there are more lines so you can add to the list. The key here is to set high expectations for yourself (because you are totally capable of attaining them!) and also to do it in a way that feels forgiving.

Like our children, we parents are human and we've made our share of mistakes. If we want to move forward with our kids, then it's really important that we let go of all of our parenting slip-ups.

As with anything you're reading in this book, as you read this list, I recommend you hang on to whatever feels right or resonates with you. Anything that doesn't feel right, go ahead and discard.

I Expect...

1. To feel better about my child

2. To model behavior that inspires my child

3. To forgive myself for any past parenting blunders

4. To spend time doing things that make me happy

5. To surround myself with uplifting people

6. To always want more

7. _____

8. _____

9. _____

10. _____

I Expect My Child...

1. To make mistakes, just like I sometimes do.

2. To want to make his/her own decisions.

3. To appreciate my support more than my control.

4. To want to be happy.

5. To hang with people he/she chooses.

6. To value his/her sense of freedom.

7. _____

8. _____

9. _____

10. _____

Experience is simply the name we give our mistakes.

OSCAR WILDE

Mistakes
How to Leverage Them

As with any expedition, if you're going to move forward on your journey, then you're going to have to discard what's not necessary or it's going to weigh you down. Specifically, when it comes to the parent-child relationship, I'm referring to *mistakes* here.

We've all made them, so there is no reason to be ashamed. And even if you're thinking right now, "Yeah, well she doesn't know how *bad* my mistakes are, or she wouldn't be writing that." To that, I'd say that I don't really care how bad your mistakes were. They're only relevant here if *you* are going to use them as your reason to not move forward.

Holding on to your mistakes would be the equivalent of taking a hiking expedition with your family. You've packed your backpack and you're headed into the mountains. You've got everything you need — or so you thought — until you figure out that all of the food in your backpack is spoiled and inedible. But then you decide that rather than dumping it in the trash, you're going to carry it for the duration, because it was your mistake and you should suffer the consequences! So, stench and all, you lug it on your back for 7 days and sleep next to it for 7 nights — and it makes for a less-than-enjoyable time for you and for your family.

You weren't born to be a perfect human being — you were born to explore and enjoy this universe. (Remember, if this statement feels good when you think it, then it's true!) So in our exploring, we're bound to slip up. Go easy on yourself when you do.

You'll notice that when you can forgive yourself for your mistakes, your kids will forgive you too — and they'll learn how to forgive themselves. Then imagine them at your age when they've had so much practice at it that when they do blunder here and there, they don't hold onto it — ever. They just chalk it up to experience and move on. What a beautiful thing!

"My father gave me the greatest gift anyone could give another person, he believed in me."

JIM VALVANO

STEP TWO
BELIEVE BIG

You've already read in this book about the importance of belief and how that old *believe it when I see it* saying is actually quite backwards. The truth is that we're not always even aware of what we believe, and that can get us into trouble.

Just for clarity sake, the definition of belief I use is: *a thought that you think over and over again.*

That's it.

Our beliefs influence our actions. They influence...

What we say

What we do

Who we do it with

Where we do it

When we do it

And because our beliefs are really only thoughts, something essential to keep in mind is: ***Our beliefs aren't necessarily true!***

The topic of beliefs, and questioning them, is one that entire books are written about. For the purposes of this book, let me say that changing my own beliefs has had a positive impact on my level of happiness — specifically, my relationships with my kids.

If you want to have a great relationship with your kids, then you have to believe it's possible. For me, the perfect question was, "Do I want to be right or do I want to be happy?" This one question motivated me to change a few things in my approach to parenting.

More than anything, I wanted to feel good about how I parented and I wanted to feel ease when I was with my kids — all of them. I also wanted them to feel comfortable when they're with me.

Questioning my current belief system is what made it possible.

As I questioned and changed certain beliefs, I felt more confident in my parenting. My kids will tell you that I loosened my reins. And, much to my delight, things began falling into place.

"Progress is impossible without change, and those who cannot change their minds cannot change anything."

GEORGE BERNARD SHAW

Change Your Mind
It's really okay!

One of my firmest parenting beliefs was that when I said something or invoked a consequence to my kids, I needed to stick to it. In other words, a deal is a deal, and that's that. If I told them that they were grounded for one week for doing something they shouldn't have done, then they didn't get un-grounded until the end of the 7th day. Period.

I made one of those deals with Nick when he began college. I told him that Mark and I would pay for his college education as long as he maintained a 3.4 grade point average. Each semester, as long as he achieved a 3.4, we would pay for the following semester. If he got below 3.4, then the next semester was on him. It was certainly doable, and he achieved even better than 3.4 that first semester in college.

Second semester was a different story. That was the semester he met Ali (now his wife) and it was also the semester he pledged for his fraternity. So his spring semester GPA slipped to 3.396.

Shortly after grades came in, we were having a large family dinner at our house and my brother P.J. was trying to coax me into paying Nick's upcoming tuition bill. Over and over, he pointed out that Nick was just.004 or (4) one-thousandths below what he needed.

"Deal's a deal," I kept responding. "If Nick was dealing with a bank, the bank would not let that slide and we're not going to either."

Without me realizing it, P.J. took Nick aside. Nick then came back to the table and offered a new deal: "How about we go double or nothing? You pay for next semester and if I don't get a 3.5 then I'll take out loans for the next two semesters?"

This was tough for me because I had "laid down the law" and my kid was asking me to break it. In my mind, going back on his consequences was a no-no, and I shouldn't do it. Aside from that, if he couldn't get a 3.4, then how was he going to earn a 3.5? And if he failed at the 3.5, then he'd owe two semesters' tuition and aside from having all that debt, what would it do to his self-esteem? (I know, such a helpful train of thought!)

In spite of what I thought was my better judgment, I accepted Nick's offer anyway. (Mark was already on board, even with the 3.396.) Making this deal was not an easy decision for me and, looking back, if it weren't for the combined persistence of my brother and my son, then I probably wouldn't have.

Nick believed in himself enough to offer the deal. No one wanted that 3.5 more than he wanted it, and he had no doubt in his mind that he would make it happen. A few months later, again Nick's grades arrived. This time they were a 3.75 GPA and he was ecstatic!

Chalk this one up as yet another learning experience for Mom. Time to add some new and better-feeling beliefs to that antiquated belief system of mine:

1. It's okay to change my mind.

2. He doesn't need me to protect him.

3. He knows what he's doing.

4. I need to let him take chances.

5. I really love watching him build self-confidence!

Exercise

Opportunities to build self-confidence are all around us. Is there something going on right now that might offer an opportunity for your child to build confidence of his or her own? Without attempting to control anything, how might you encourage him/her to take a chance on something that has meaning? How can you step aside and support your child while he or she is in control?

"It is the spectator, and not life, that art really mirrors."

OSCAR WILDE

Spectator Preference
Rowdy insult guy or supportive cheerleader?

As I mentioned in the beginning of this book, I was not a typical little girl. Unlike the rest of the girls in the neighborhood who were playing with Barbie dolls and learning to make crafts, and do hair, I was playing football, baseball, and basketball with the boys.

My father loved telling the story about one of the times when I was grounded and one of the boys in the neighborhood came to the door asking him if Lisa could please come out to play because they needed a quarterback.

Needless to say, for me, having daughters came with added challenges. I used to think that God was playing a big trick on me, and that having girls was my payment for being the rebel that I was as a teen. I thought that there was a skill set that I was lacking and that my girls would suffer because of it.

Again, this was far from the truth.

What I learned through my girly-girl daughters was that my girls did not need me to teach them how to do girly things, or even how to earn A's in school. They were perfectly capable of learning about what interested them — because they had no reason to believe they couldn't — and all they really needed me to provide was the encouragement and support.

In other words, rather than me being their coach who taught them skills, they learned to develop their own skills and wanted me to cheer them on.

Ponytails, buns, dresses, dolls, dance, and etiquette were so far out of my realm that it just seemed easier to agree with their choices, rather than suggest something I really knew nothing about.

The strategy worked so well with girly-girl issues. If only I'd realized sooner that this same hands-off approach could work in other areas just as well.

Kids want our support. They want to know that we believe in them. They want to meet and exceed the expectations we have for them. And they are constantly aware of the feedback we offer. They know we're watching. They listen for our feedback and they feel it.

Imagine you're out there in front of a few hundred spectators, playing a sport you enjoy. You really want to demonstrate the peak performance you're capable of. You're giving it your all — focusing on the game, observing your opponent(s) and what they're doing — all while anticipating your next move and then quickly making it. While all this is going on, you can't help but hear the lively comments coming from the crowd.

Which kind of comments do you find most helpful and motivating, the ones that help you bring on your peak performance? Which loud spectators do you want to hear more from?

Is it easier to make your best moves while listening to comments that recognize what you're doing right? Or do you appreciate criticism from those who point out where you've slipped up?

Your response to these questions may be different from what mine would be and they're worth noting. But whatever *your* response is, these are great questions to ask your kids.

They're not only really good questions, just asking your kids which type of spectator they prefer lets them know that you're interested in knowing what they think… that you *want* to know what they find helpful and you *want* to help them succeed. You want them to realize their peak performance.

Of course, once you know their spectator preference, then the pressure is on *you* to give them what they want and need. Let me be the first to say, "You got this!"

Exercise

The purpose of this exercise is not to judge, only to observe. The next time you're at a sporting event, quietly take notice of the spectators around you. Pay special attention to their comments. Pick a few close by whose comments you can compare and contrast. Notice what they say to and about their children and also to and about others. If the children can hear them, how do the kids respond? How would you respond to these same comments if they were directed toward you?

Your experience of this exercise need not be shared with anyone. Its sole purpose is for your information and clarity only, and the reason it's helpful is because the role of *spectator* is one of those roles that we learn by watching those around us. As with many things, it seems more natural to do what other people are doing.

There's a lot of wisdom to be gained from being a spectator among the spectators. Distinguishing the helpful and unhelpful comments will let you become the spectator you intentionally want to be — rather than the spectator it's easier to become by blending in.

One last note: Of course, you are a spectator at your child's sporting events and you're also a spectator of everything he or she does in life. Whatever works best for your child on the field is likely to work best in all areas of his or her life.

"The thing always happens that you really believe in; and the belief in a thing makes it happen."

FRANK LLOYD WRIGHT

Lose the Doubt
It'll make better things possible.

Let me begin this segment by telling you that this next story has absolutely nothing to do with kids or parenting — and it has everything to do with why I believe so strongly that our beliefs about anything (including our kids) actually set the stage for what ends up happening.

In March of 2009, my husband and I were lucky to be part of a group of over four hundred people invited by a large company (one of my husband's vendors) to attend the Big East basketball tournament in New York City's Madison Square Garden. If you're a basketball junkie, then you may already know that that was the year Syracuse (our home team) beat Connecticut in six overtimes.

Syracuse then won the following night's game and was set to play the championship game. On the morning of the championship game, as my husband and I were heading to Starbucks for our daily fix, I mentioned to him that I thought his brother and our sister-in-law would love to join us for that evening's game. He quickly pointed out that the game was a sell-out and that the vendor who gave us our tickets was also trying unsuccessfully to get two more tickets for his own family members.

I heard what Mark said, and then I called my brother-in-law and invited him and his wife to come to the game. I was honest. I told him that I didn't have tickets yet and there weren't any for sale, but I would get them and they'd be free.

And when I got them, I told him I'd call and let them know to come into the city and meet us.

Both Mark and Mike thought I was a little nuts, but they went along with it and Mike agreed he and Veronica would meet us in the city if I got the tickets.

A couple hours later, Mark and I stopped into the Brooklyn Diner and met the daughter of a woman we know from Syracuse. We were telling this young lady that we were going to the Syracuse game that night and she said she would have loved to go, but she couldn't get tickets.

I told her I didn't have extra tickets but I was going to get some free ones. So I invited her to come. At this point, Mark was getting a little annoyed because he had already called a few people for me and he was striking out on extra tickets — let alone free ones. But I asked the girl for her number and told her I'd call when I had the tickets.

Mark and I had a terrific day in the city. We got last-minute sixth-row-center stage seats to a Jane Fonda play where I sat right next to college football Hall-of-Famer Johnny Majors. Besides being a really great guy, Johnny was a former football coach at Pittsburgh who had coached a neighbor of ours from Syracuse. So I told him we were going to the Syracuse basketball game that night and asked if he wanted to come. But he and his wife already had plans.

After the play, Mark and I headed back to the hotel to freshen up for dinner and then the game. I also needed to find those tickets. I knew they existed and all I had to do was find them. Since we were part of a large group, I dragged Mark up to the hospitality room where we saw a guy locking the door of that room behind him.

I told the guy I needed four tickets to that night's game and asked if he knew where I could get them. He chuckled, said there weren't any and wished me luck.

Mark and I then went to our room and got ready to head over to Madison Square Garden. When we came down to meet the group in our hotel lobby, the guy from the hospitality room walked by and asked if I'd gotten any tickets. I told him I hadn't, and again asked if he'd let me know if he found any.

It was getting close to game time when we were at the Garden for a little pre-game dinner when hospitality guy came up to me in the buffet line and again asked if I'd found those tickets. He had someone with him this time — a man who asked me how many tickets I wanted, because he happened to have some. The man kindly handed me four tickets and, of course, they were free!

I get goose bumps every time I think of this story! That morning I had absolutely no idea where those tickets would come from, but I knew they existed and I knew that they would come to me.

As I mentioned, this story has absolutely nothing to do with kids or parenting, but, for me, it was a deciding moment and is something that helps me tremendously when it comes to making decisions regarding my kids. This experience is what strongly convinced me that dropping my doubt and following my instincts is what allows amazing things happen.

Unlike my previous belief that I needed to *force* things to happen, *allowing* things to happen is much easier, more fun, and super exciting!

Exercise

Is there something (anything) you *want* to believe about your child, but you're not there yet? Every time you think about this thing, you think of all the reasons why this is just not possible for this particular kid. Other people might agree with you on this, too — even the professionals you look to for advice. They mean well. They just don't want you to get your hopes up too high and then be let down by reality.

Still, I invite you to think about the possibility of this thing happening for your child. Think about one reason why it could happen. Think about that one reason and entertain the notion that there may even be another reason that you're not yet aware of that might also make this possible. Then wonder what that second reason could possibly be. Just wonder about it without trying to force it to happen. Just *know* that it could.

Know that there is at least one way that this great thing you want for your child could actually happen. See yourself being fascinated when it appears. How will you recognize it? Feel that humungous smile on your face as you tell others that you knew it could happen. What will you tell them? Imagine the delight on your child's face when he or she experiences it.

See it all in your imagination and feel it in your body. Notice the connection between your imagination and how your body feels. Notice what hope feels like. Breathe it in and let it fill your heart.

Note: Doing this exercise will help you focus on possibility. As you do, you take your focus off any doubts.

"To me luxury is to be at home with my daughter, and the occasional massage doesn't hurt."

OLIVIA NEWTON-JOHN

STEP THREE
CHILL OUT

Time For You
And it's about time!

I have to admit this is my favorite part of the book, and I hope it's yours too!

It's my favorite because it's where I get to write about excitement for *you*. You're a parent, yes, but you're also a real, live person with real, live desires that matter. With kids added to your list of responsibilities, you often put yourself on the proverbial back burner.

With more and more on your plate, you figure that something has to give. If that something is you, then at least you don't have to listen to someone else complain that they aren't getting what they need from you. Right? Doesn't it just seem easier sometimes to forget about yourself and your needs?

You think:

> *I'll take care of myself later.*
>
> *I can wait.*
>
> *It's only me.*

I'm tough.

I can handle it.

Just let me take care of these other people first.

What ends up happening is that a very long time (sometimes forever) goes by before you ever tend to your own needs!

You, the very person who goes out of your way to be sure that your family has food to eat, clothes to wear, supplies for school, an audience to perform in front of, and rides to practice, will not think twice about missing something you enjoy doing for yourself.

You're not the only one. A lot of us think (thought) there's something noble about being self-less while we cater to others and their desires.

I know this because I lived it and I've coached others who did it, too. There is nothing wrong with living this way, so long as you don't begin resenting the very people whose needs you place above your own.

When that happens, it's time for a self-exam where you sit down and ask yourself what *you* need. And if you're already saying that you don't have time for this, then that's how you know you're long overdue.

If you wait until you "have time" to do something for yourself, then you'll never do it, because something will always come up that you can do for someone else. And, of course, that results in even less free time for you.

Aside from the fact that your body, mind, and spirit crave your attention, how about tending to your own needs simply because you'll feel better when you do? And when you feel better, every aspect of your life gets better. You become increasingly happier and you can't help but spread more happiness to those around you, including your kids.

A myriad of scientific evidence exists that proves emotions are contagious — which is why it makes perfect sense to identify which emotions you're feeling, just so you can get a good grip on what you're sharing with the people around you.

If you think that wearing a smile on your face will mask the true emotions you're feeling, you may want to re-think that one. If you're feeling tired, angry, or overwhelmed, even if you're not aware of what you're feeling — that smile is not fooling your kids.

You know this is true, because you can sense emotions in other people, too. You can feel when someone's not happy, even if they don't verbalize it. You can tell that something's not right, and you can feel the masked tension affecting others in the room.

When you practice good self-care, you're taking responsibility for your own happiness and you're also taking responsibility for the vibe you put out to others. You know that your emotions are contagious and you're being sure to share good ones.

As a parent who didn't always prioritize self-care, and as someone who now appreciates its many benefits, I want to spend the remainder of this book on things you can do that will feel great to you and benefit your kids at the same time.

As always, there are no rights and wrongs here — only *feels good* and *doesn't feel good*.

When you *feel* better, you *do* better... and you enjoy what you're doing. It's very different from doing things just because you think you're *supposed* to do them.

I have a friend who says that when she reads a book, her hope is that she can find just one nugget of helpful information inside. Then she'll take that one nugget and run with it.

Of course, I hope you find even more than one nugget in this book, but if you were going to find just one, I would recommend it be this: **Make your own happiness your greatest priority.**

You may be having the same reaction many of my clients have when I lay this one on them. You're probably thinking that living this way is selfish and that kids lose out when their parents prioritize their own happiness. Fair assumption, but let's look at this further.

If a parent prioritizes her own happiness and is happy the majority of the time, then what is the dominant emotion she is sharing with her family? Yes — happiness!

And, in addition to sharing positive emotions, she is also teaching her kids how to prioritize their own happiness. She's teaching them that it's not up to their parents or friends or teachers or coaches or partners or bosses or anyone else to make them happy. It's up to *them*. This is a powerful lesson — one that's challenging for adults to learn, because we learned to do things differently a while back, maybe all our lives. But it is possible to learn now and all it takes is some focus and consistency.

Prioritizing your own happiness is something anyone can learn, at whatever age, and when you do, you show your kids (and others) how it's done. As with everything, it starts in your mind.

When you think about being happy and things that truly make you happy, you have to be happy — because that's how this universe works. The more you think this way, the easier it becomes and the more naturally happy you are.

With *happy* on your mind, it's also on your radar — which means that more happiness is what your radar will detect.

This next exercise will help you kick off your own happiness radar campaign.

Exercise

Below is a list of statements, some of which may feel really good and true for you. Some of which may not. The purpose of this list is to offer examples of thoughts you may want to adapt that will help you increase your own happiness. You can add to and subtract from the list, with the sole purpose of making the list your own. If a statement feels good to you, then keep it. If you disagree with the statement, modify or delete it entirely.

- I like feeling happy.

- I like that I can create my own happiness with my thoughts.

- I have the ability to choose happy thoughts throughout my day.

- The more I focus on creating happiness, the more natural it will become.

- I like that I can make myself happy just by thinking certain thoughts.

- Appreciating certain things and people feels good to me.

- The more I find to appreciate in people and things, the better I feel.

- I could get really good at this appreciation thing.

- I can even find things to appreciate in people and things that used to annoy me.

- I like choosing my thoughts deliberately.

- Being deliberate with my thoughts helps me feel more in control.

- I like doing things that interest me.

- I can probably find time in my day just for me.

- I get excited about doing more of what I love.

- It's so good that my kids get to see me take responsibility for my happiness.

- My kids are learning how to be happy — just by watching me!

Note: Reading through your list regularly will help you tune into whatever your idea of *happy* is! For best results, update your happiness list regularly and watch your happiness grow.

"It's not your job to like me.
It's mine."

BYRON KATIE

Self-Kindness
Because it feels better.

Have you noticed the chatter going on inside your head lately? By *chatter*, I mean the statements you think *about* yourself and even *at* yourself. Scientists say that, on average, we think 60,000 thoughts each day. So I did the math. Assuming we're awake for 18 of those hours — that's 3,333 thoughts per hour, and over 55 per minute!

It goes without saying that we can't possibly be aware of all the thoughts we have, and it's certainly not possible to police every single one.

But these thoughts we think are not only *affecting* the emotions we feel, they actually *cause* them — and these are the very same emotions we give off to the people around us.

Being kind to ourselves, starting with our thoughts, is the best thing we can do for ourselves, and it doesn't take any *more* time in our schedules. It's more a matter of redirection of thoughts than adding more thoughts — and doing it on purpose.

One of the best ways to improve your self-care is to *intentionally* think good thoughts about yourself. As you begin getting intentional in your thinking, the old self-deprecating thoughts will still pop up. Just notice them if they do and dismiss them. You might even tell them that they're not helpful to you anymore and that you've got some new and better-feeling ways to think about yourself.

As you stay consistent with your new, intentional patterns of thought, they become your default way of thinking. You'll think less trash about yourself, and you'll enjoy the experience of having thoughts that are more aligned with the spirit of who you really are.

Getting intentional with your self-talk is a process that does not happen overnight, but I guarantee that if you stay consistent with the practice, the rewards are many and they will continue to grow.

As you think more positively about yourself, about your character and unique qualities, knowing that you are enough just as you are right now, then you will begin to notice proof in your life that demonstrates that and more.

Somehow, we fall into a trap where we compare ourselves with people we believe are doing really well in certain arenas that we'd like to do well in. And, of course, we see ourselves coming up on the short end of the stick. We see them having more than we have and then we berate ourselves for not keeping up.

All along, we do this without any idea of how those people feel on the inside. We make our observations from the outside, and assume they're happy with their results and life feels perfect to them. Then we begin the litany of things we did wrong that prevented us from having those very things that we want.

I think we've all been there. Eventually, there comes a time when you decide to pack it in and holler *ENOUGH! That's enough beating myself up! That's enough with wasting my time entertaining crappy-feeling thoughts! Sign me up for a better way!*

Exercise

Interested in a few ideas on how to get intentional with your self-talk? You might consider these:

- I like learning new and interesting things.

- I like finding new ways to grow.

- I want to share positive emotions with people.

- I have some really fine qualities.

- I deserve to be happy.

- The idea of taking time for myself feels good to me.

- It feels better when I think kind thoughts about myself.

- I don't need other people's approval.

- I only need my own approval, and I am learning how to give it.

- What other people achieve really has nothing to do with me.

- I can choose to be inspired by what other people have.

- If someone else can figure out how to do something, then I can figure it out too.

- There is no benefit to being hard on myself, but there is a benefit to going easy.

- Good-feeling self-talk inspires me to take positive action.

- Thinking deliberately lets me create a more helpful mindset.

For best results, add to, subtract from, and update this list to give it your own personalized touches. Reading through your list regularly will help you develop an internal dialogue that appreciates you just the way you are!

"You can search throughout the entire universe for someone who is more deserving of your love and affection than you are yourself, and that person is not to be found anywhere. You yourself, as much as anybody in the entire universe deserve your love and affection."

BUDDHA

What Do You Want?
Whatever it is, you deserve it!

One of the best things about thinking deliberately is that you get to create whatever you want. When you intentionally choose your thoughts, you're not caught up in the old thoughts that used to limit you and weigh down your efforts.

When you think deliberately about something you want, you think of the reasons why *you can* have it, not why you can't.

As a parent, it's very easy to get caught up in the role of *parent* and give no attention to who you are as a person.

As you move into this next exercise, let me give you one warning: Making the shift toward designing (or redesigning) the person you want to be is known to begin as challenging, and eventually become terribly exciting!

Exercise

If you could change something about one of the following areas of your life, which area would you want to change first?

a. Career

b. Relationships

c. Finances

d. Health

Specifically, what change would you like to create?

_____

_____

_____

How long have you wanted to make this change?

_____

How long are you willing to wait before making this happen? _____

Describe what it will look like when this change happens. What will be different? What will you see, hear, taste, touch, and smell that will let you know this change has occurred?

_____

_____

_____

Name one thing you could do that would help things move in a forward direction?

_____

Name the feeling you would have if this change happened today? _____

_____

List three things you could commit to doing on a regular basis that will give you that same feeling.

1. _____

2. _____

3. _____

What thoughts can you think about where you are right now (in relation to where you want to be) that will allow you to feel better about being right where you are? For example:

1. There's a certain level of comfort in being where I am.

2. I know I don't have to stay here forever.

3. I have the ability to change this when I'm ready.

4. I have done harder things than this before.

5. What's good about where I am now is that it lets me

_____

6. I don't have to have all the answers right now.

7. I can move in increments toward what I want.

8. I'm always going to want more for myself.

9. Moving toward what I want keeps things interesting for me.

Now it's your turn:

_____

_____

_____

_____

_____

You may find that the previous exercise helped you gain all the clarity you needed to move forward into the life of your dreams. If this is the case, please know that you are a very rare and inspiring individual and I would love to hear the story on how you did this so quickly. So please email me at lisa@lisacavallaro.com and share!

On the other hand, if you find that you have more questions than answers, you would be considered among the majority. This exercise is designed to help you generate ideas that point you in a general direction. Even if you're not sure what your next forward steps will be, just know that your improved clarity is absolutely a helpful first step. Consistent practice of the tools in this section can help you take it from here.

"When you arise in the morning, think of what a precious privilege it is to be alive — to breathe, to think, to enjoy, to love."

MARCUS AURELIUS

A Morning Practice
Start your day strong!

As I mentioned in the beginning of this section, this part of the book where we spend time on the importance of regular self-care is my favorite part. I like writing and talking about self-care because time spent taking care of our selves is time spent feeling good — and it feels good just thinking about it. Oh, the many benefits of great self-care!

When we feel good, we know it. We feel it in our minds and our bodies, too. The people who surround us know it, because we broadcast it out in the energy we share with them. I mentioned earlier about our emotions being contagious and the exact same thing happens when it comes to feeling good.

When I first learned that emotions carry energy, it seemed a little weird. But the more I thought about it, the more I realized that it does make perfect sense. We all know what it is to feel someone's "vibe." We've all said or thought, "I get a bad vibe from that person," or, "She's got awesome energy."

It's hard to describe the energy in visual terms because we can't see it. But you know what I'm talking about because you've experienced it. You've picked up on people's energy without having to use your senses or your active mind to do it.

So you know the energy is there, because somehow you connect with it even though to the eye it's invisible. You've undoubtedly had experiences with good vibes and not-so-good ones. You can tell the difference by how they *feel* to you.

You know, too, that good vibes are fun to be around and make you want more — like being at a great concert with music that makes you feel amazing. After the last song, you clap, hoot, and holler so the band will come back and play just one more song to keep the vibration going. By the time that very last song is over, you're flowing a vibe that feels awesome.

So it might not be possible to attend mind-blowing concerts every day, but it is possible to start your day out flowing a vibration that feels good while it sets the stage for more good things to come.

Consider this your morning practice — a time each morning that you dedicate to *you*. During this time, you do whatever floats your boat and brings you into alignment with your best energy.

When my kids were younger, morning practice for me was exercise. I liked getting up long before them so that I could get in a good sweat and a shower before they began their day. After a few years, though, it seemed I needed more.

I still love and appreciate the benefits of regular exercise, but several years ago, I found that it wasn't enough to really get me feeling great in the morning. It's funny how adding a simple ten-minute morning practice made a huge difference for me.

I define morning practice as an activity that points you in the direction you want to go each day. The exact practice is different for different people, and it can also change periodically — whenever you want to change it.

What can a morning practice do for you? It's probably a safe bet to say that a morning practice can help you accomplish anything. Aside from making you feel better, a morning practice can help you reach whatever goals you've set for yourself by helping you create and maintain the right focus.

So many times, the only reason we don't achieve certain goals is because we have some inner belief that says we're not capable of attaining them. A morning practice that includes finding thoughts in alignment with your goals will diminish the power of whatever old limiting beliefs you may have had.

Morning practice is your time. It's a short while that you get to spend alone, doing something that aligns your energy in whatever way you need it to be aligned, so that you can get the most from your day ahead. Some days you may be more focused on fun with the family — just loosening up and relaxing. Other days you might find it helpful to use your morning practice to prepare for a difficult meeting or speech in front of a large audience.

No matter the schedule for your day, taking time to align your energy is time well spent — because no matter what you have going on, aligned energy will allow you to act in ways that support the goals you've set for yourself.

You can use your morning practice to help you align your energy with regard to your relationships, finances, career, or health. The list goes on and on. If you have thoughts on it, then you can align your energy on it.

What works best for my morning practice is something called *visualization*. The practice has been around for a long time, and you've probably even heard in the news about certain athletes and performers who use it to achieve their best results. Maybe you've used it yourself. (I used it when I played high school sports, but I had no idea what it was called or even the power that it could have outside of sports. All I knew is that it really lit me up and got me ready for game time!)

I highly recommend visualization for parents. Here's why:

- It jump-starts your day in a positive way.

- It feels good.

- It sets the stage for what you notice throughout your day.

- With consistency, you will amaze yourself and those around you.

- You can use visualization to make parenting easier.

- You can use visualization to improve the parent-child relationship.

- It's the exact opposite of worry, which never helps.

My very non-technical, simplified definition of visualization is *something you create in your mind that allows you to experience it happening before it actually happens*. You create a movie where you actually see things that you want to happen come to life in your mind. You see, hear, touch, smell, and taste them right in your imagination — and since it's something you want to happen, you feel great as you're experiencing it.

You get to write the script and you get to direct the movie. The perfect use of thought: seeing things happen that you *want* to happen!

Some may consider this to be daydreaming or escaping reality and maybe it is. I just call it amazingly helpful. Remember, what we're going for here is a *feeling* that you get to feel for one reason only: because it feels good. Anything that feels good is adding to your vibration because it carries with it the potential to make your life even better.

Science has proven that even if these good-feeling things (people, objects, experiences) are only in your imagination, they still affect your vibration. This is huge!

As scientist and author Gregg Braden says in his book *The Divine Matrix*, "Like attracts like...," so if you're feeling the vibration of what you want to have happen in your life, then you're in a better position to attract it.

Exercise
Creating A Morning Practice That Lights You Up

Find a special, quiet space in your home that you can visit each morning.

- Go to your quiet space shortly after waking up, or at a time that feels best to you. Plan on visualizing for approximately ten minutes.

- Wear comfortable clothes and sit comfortably.

- Close your eyes and set an intention. Your intention may be something general, such as *Today is my best day yet!* Or it might be more specific, such as *I see my child doing things that make me proud.*

- Describe your intention as it unfolds in your mind. For instance, describe what you see as you live your best day yet. Who is there with you? What are you doing? What outfit are you wearing? Where are you? What do you hear? What are you saying? Are there other sounds? Is someone else speaking? Are you holding or touching anything? Is your body temperature warmer or colder? Are you standing, sitting, walking, or riding? What do you smell? What emotions do you feel? How intense are the emotions? In other words, create what you want to happen with as much clarity as you can and be sure to see yourself in there. You're not watching it from the sidelines — you are experiencing it fully with all of your senses.

- If anything negative or thoughts on other topics come to mind, no worries — just bring your mind back to visualizing.

- Consistency is key. If you miss a day or two or thirty, no worries. Just resume as soon as you can.

"I don't remember who said this, but there really are places in the heart you don't even know exist until you love a child."

ANNE LAMOTT

CONCLUSION
SAVOR IT ALL!

It's probably no coincidence that I find myself writing this book during a summer of many joyous family events. Nick was married in May. Dina graduated high school in June. And Marisa was married on the Fourth of July.

Still feeling remnants of the rush of joy this last year has brought, I look back with gratitude on what I refer to as my struggle years. They may have been torturous at the time, but when I think of all the growth I got to experience because of them, I am eternally thankful for every bit of it.

Marisa's wedding was two weeks ago. Much to my surprise, she invited not only my husband to speak at her reception; she also invited me. I was honored for two reasons: in my experience, it was only the father who offered the toast at his daughter's wedding, and also because Marisa's gesture spoke volumes about how far our relationship has come.

Marisa also gave me a hand-written note the day before her wedding. I'm sure she'd be happy to know that I'm sharing it here. The front of the card had this quote from Mark Twain: "My mother had a great deal of trouble with me but, I think she enjoyed it." Inside it she wrote:

"Mom, How perfect is this card?? I can't believe the big day is finally here! I feel so fortunate and so grateful for the wedding of my dreams. Thank you for everything you have done for me, not only for the wedding, but for my entire life.

I cherish all the special times and memories we share together and look forward to what the future brings.

If you had asked me 10 years ago if I thought my mother would be my best friend I would have said you were crazy, but now I couldn't agree more and I couldn't imagine it any other way.

I'll always be your little girl and best friend.

Love you Always,

Marisa

There is not one thing in this world that could have made me more proud in that moment! Marisa's words were especially touching because neither one of us pretends that our battles didn't exist. Instead, we refer to them often. Sometimes jokingly, but always with gratitude for where they've brought us.

I had already written my speech for Marisa's wedding toast, and although I saved my words for the next day, how appropriate it was that we were both thinking the same thing on that special occasion. In my toast at Marisa's wedding, I thanked her for being the best teacher I've ever had.

As Helen Hayes said, "Childhood is a very short season." Now that my youngest is 18 years old, I'll second that. Even though there were days when it didn't seem so, today it feels like it all went by in a blink.

Before jumping into this thing called parenthood, I thought it was my responsibility to teach my kids all I knew. Luckily for them, I learned better. Luckily for me, my kids came with lessons of their own:

- I learned that parenting is harder than I thought.

- I learned that parenting is also easier than I thought.

- I learned that I was the one who made it hard.

- And I was the one who finally let it get easier.

- By their very nature, kids are brilliant.

- And they're good.

- And they're wise.

- And they have the strength and wisdom they need to get them where they need to go.

As Nick, Marisa, and Dina all demonstrated, kids are also very forgiving.

Another huge lesson I learned is that it's never too late.

It's never too late to change anything.

And it's never too late to change how you parent.

Take it from someone who learned the hard way, if you look at your child's behavior as nothing more than a reflection of how you view them, just change how you view them, and you will notice different things.

As you hold high expectations for your child, believe in his or her abilities, and add to your own sense of joy, I promise you there will come a day when you look back with gratitude for whatever challenges your child has brought you.

Along with that gratitude, you will feel a deep sense of pride — because you didn't waste your time trying to force your change on someone else. Instead, you cared enough to make changes in your own life and you provided your kids with an example of how to increase their own sense of joy — and all your kids needed to do was *watch*!

ABOUT THE
AUTHOR

Lisa Cavallaro is the founder of Aim High & Lead, co-author of Ten Life Skills Never Taught But Totally Essential to Happy Living, and blogger with the Huffington Post. While moving through what she calls her "struggle years" with her middle child, Lisa learned that parenting is one of the many life circumstances that got easier as she let it. In mastering a simple re-focusing technique, Lisa learned how to build stronger and more enjoyable relationships with her kids.

After a successful 20-year business career, Lisa pursued a master's degree centered in systems and relationships, while utilizing her skills as a school counselor in local K-8 schools. She went on to further her training, earning master certifications in coaching, weight loss coaching, and Reiki and launched her coaching business in 2007.

Lisa's 3-step method offers a simplified, easy to adapt framework that can be applied to all aspects of life. This technique is what made the greatest difference in dealing with her own daughter's defiant behavior and is the same technique she uses with the hundreds of clients she has helped throughout the years. Working with parents, teachers and school districts, Lisa delivers practical strategies designed to complement the child's learning process. She lives in Syracuse, NY with her husband and family.

Email Lisa at: lisa@lisacavallaro.com

Follow her blog: huffingtonpost.com/lisa-cavallaro/

difference press

Difference Press offers solopreneurs, including life coaches, healers, consultants, and community leaders, a comprehensive solution to get their books written, published, and promoted. A boutique-style alternative to self-publishing, Difference Press boasts a fair and easy-to-understand profit structure, low-priced author copies, and author-friendly contract terms. Its founder, Dr. Angela Lauria, has been bringing to life the literary ventures of hundreds of authors -in-transformation since 1994.

YOUR DELICIOUS BOOK

Your Delicious Book is a trailblazing program for aspiring authors who want to create a non-fiction book that becomes a platform for growing their business or communicating their message to the world in a way that creates a difference in the lives of others.

In a market where hundreds of thousands books are published every year and never heard from again, all of The Author Incubator participants have bestsellers that are actively changing lives and making a difference. The program, supported by quarterly Difference Press book-marketing summits, has a proven track record of helping aspiring authors write books that matter. Our team will hold your hand from idea to impact, showing you how to write a book, what elements must be present in your book for it to deliver the results you need, and how to meet the needs of your readers. We give you all the editing, design, and technical support you need to ensure a high-quality book published to the Kindle platform. Plus, authors in the program are connected to a powerful community of authors-in-transformation and published bestselling authors.

TACKLING THE TECHNICAL ASPECTS OF PUBLISHING

The comprehensive coaching, editing, design, publishing, and marketing services offered by Difference Press mean that your book will be edited by a pro, designed by an experienced graphic artist, and published digitally and in print by publishing industry experts. We handle all of the technical aspects of your book's creation so you can spend more of your time focusing on your business.

APPLY TO WRITE WITH US

To submit an application to our acquisitions team visit www.YourDeliciousBook.com.

OTHER BOOKS BY DIFFERENCE PRESS

*Confessions of an
Unlikely Runner:
A Guide to Racing
and Obstacle
Courses for the
Averagely Fit and
Halfway Dedicated*

by Dana L. Ayers

*Matter: How to
Find Meaningful
Work That's
Right for You and
Your Family*

by Caroline
Greene

*Reclaiming
Wholeness: Letting
Your Light Shine
Even If You're
Scared to Be Seen*

by Kimberlie
Chenoweth

*The Well-Crafted
Mom: How to
Make Time for
Yourself and Your
Creativity within
the Midst of
Motherhood*

by Kathleen
Harper

*Lifestyle Design for
a Champagne Life:
Find Out Why the
Law of Attraction
Isn't Working,
Learn the Secret to
Lifestyle Design,
and Create Your
Champagne Life*

by Cassie Parks

*No More Drama:
How to Make
Peace with Your
Defiant Kid*

by Lisa Cavallaro

*The Nurse
Practitioner's Bag:
Become a Healer,
Make a Difference,
and Create the
Career of Your
Dreams*

by Nancy Brook

*Farm Girl
Leaves Home:
An American
Narrative of
Inspiration and
Transformation*

by Margaret
Fletcher

Whoops! I Forgot to Achieve My Potential

by Maggie Huffman

Only 10s: Using Distraction to Get the Right Things Done

by Mark Silverman

The Inside Guide to MS: How to Survive a New Diagnosis When Your Whole Life Changes (And You Just Want to Go Home)

by Andrea Hanson

Lee & Me: What I Learned from Parenting a Child with Adverse Childhood Experiences

by Wendy Gauntner

The Peaceful Daughter's Guide to Separating from A Difficult Mother: Freeing Yourself From The Guilt, Anger, Resentment and Bitterness

by Karen C. L. Anderson

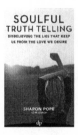

Soulful Truth Telling: Disbelieving the Lies That Keep Us From the Love We Desire

by Sharon Pope

Personal Finance That Doesn't Suck: A 5-step Guide to Quit Budgeting, Start Wealth Building and Get the Most from Your Money

by Mindy Crary

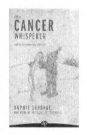

The Cancer Whisperer: How to Let Cancer Heal Your Life

by Sophie Sabbage

20534847R00090

Made in the USA
San Bernardino, CA
28 December 2018